The Little Book of INTRODVERTED THOUGHTS

Volume 3

Talisha A. Matheson

ISBN: 978-1-7777453-8-7

Disclaimer: These quotes are the intellectual property taken from published and unpublished works of The Inspired Introvert. All other quotes are credited to the best of my knowledge.

Dear Reader,

Welcome to Volume 3, the final installment in ***The Little Book of Introverted Thoughts****.* *This book is a collection of random thoughts, encouragements, reflections, and inspiration. So, turn the page, find a quote that speaks to you and let its message permeate the corners of your mind to start and keep the conversations going.*

Be Inspired!

Fitting someone into your schedule and *making time* **is different.**

We can't *heal* from it
if we don't admit
there is *something*
to heal from.

Unmonitored
access
breeds
blindness.

— *RC Blake*

God **plants the seed;**
our job is to water it.
He will provide the sun
until it's *time* **to harvest.**

Refusing **to choose**
is a *choice.*

The *silence*
will always disturb you
if you can't find *peace*
in the noise.

You know
you have *changed*
when you no longer
fear **the results**
of asking God
to *remove* **people**
from your life.

The *quietest* voice
is the *loudest*
in the room.

Being *humble*
will cure you
of the need
to *always* be right.

Be an *observer* of your negative thoughts. They do not *define* you.

— Unknown

Be with someone who is *sure* about you when you are *unsure* about yourself.

We can't *heal* from it if we don't *talk* about it.

When we don't *value* our relationship with *ourselves*, we don't see the value of *relationships* with others.

When they
treat *you*
like you
don't *matter,*
remember who
Created **you.**

Don't let
the *visitors*
in your life
become *squatters.*

Reminder:
When you die,
your job
will *replace* **you.**
Your family and
loved ones can't.
Adjust your *priorities.*

You can't talk your *way* out of a problem that you *behaved* your way into.

— *Stephen R. Covey*

The *moment*
we consider ourselves
to be self-made
is the moment
we *place* ourselves
above God.

Some things
happen **on** *purpose*
for a purpose.

Sometimes,
we are so busy
protecting **ourselves**
that we fail to realize
we are *hurting* **others.**

In the end,

we all

become stories.

— Unknown

Our *trials*
and tribulations
are there to *shape* **us,**
not *condemn* **us.**

Do you use your pain to *define* you, or do you *grow* from it?

Forgiven
people
should be
forgiving
people.

— harvest.org

Pay *attention*
to where people
place **you.**
Are you in the circle
of *importance*
or on the sidelines
of *convenience?*

People **don't care what you know until they know you** *care.*

— *With the Perrys*

To have a *healthy relationship,* **you must first believe it** *exists.*

— @Bobby_chandler

Stop *pouring* **into bottomless vessels.**

The absence of *God* in your relationship is like *watering* soil without any seeds and expecting *growth.*

Remember
who created you
when *feelings*
of insignificance
surrounds you.

When we *focus*
on what we lack,
we miss the *abundance*
of *blessings* around us.

Not everyone will see the *essence* of who you are. Stop *waiting* for them to gain sight.

Finding the *courage*
to love after heartbreak
is a *gangster* **move.**

We don't *appreciate*
the presence of
God until we are
at the bottom,
and He is the only one
reaching down
to pull us up.

Trauma **happens to us,**
but healing is a *choice.*

— Tony Gaskins

Heal **so interactions with genuine souls never feel like a** *threat.*

Not *everyone* **is meant to be in every** *season* **of your life.**

The Man
that *finds* **his voice,**
finds his *way.*

— Jay Barnet

Identify the *participants* **and** *spectators* **in your life.**

Refrain from *expecting* people to fit into your *prefabricated* box.

Why are you able to *speak* life into others, but not speak it to your *reflection*?

— *Dr. Natasha*

There is a *difference* between the eyes *wandering* and the heart making a *home* elsewhere.

Be cautious of *hurt* that is *camouflaged* as strength.

— *Unknown*

Being healthy is not just about the body. It's about your mind,
body **and** *soul.*

If anyone can *offend* you, anyone can *own* you.

— *Judge Lynn Toler*

Time **doesn't heal all wounds.**
Growth **does.**

— *Pastor James Edwards*

When *we* focus
on the pain,
we never *recover*.

You are *uniquely*
and
purposefully **made.**

— *The Bible*

Toxic *communication* sounds good because it *resonates* with the unhealed parts of you.

Healing
is a journey.
Wholeness
is a destination.

— *Dr. Jay Barnett*

The *words* you speak become the house you *live* in.

— *Hafiz*

Heartbreak is
inevitable.
Healing is
a choice.

Love **recognizes no barriers. It jumps hurdles, leaps fences, penetrates walls to arrive at its** *destination* **full of hope.**

— *Maya Angelou*

The *universe* didn't create you, *God* did.

Common **sense**
should not
be *controversial.*

— *Dee1*

Your *future*
needs you.
Your *past* **doesn't.**

— *m.r.*

Communication **is to a relationship like** *oxygen* **is to life.**

— *Tony Gaskins*

Loneliness
destroys the soul.
Solitude
refreshes it.

— Ken Claytor

At some point, you must *stop apologizing* **and do better.**

To *love* and be loved is to *feel* the sun from both sides.

— David Viscott

It's okay
to say *no* to those
who have always
benefited from
your yes.

We all have *time.*
Who and what
we give it to is
always **a choice.**

Sight **is a function of the eyes, but** *vision* **is a function of the heart**

— *Myles Munroe*

Stop giving people an *all-access* pass to you when they only deserve a *preview*.

Stop *expecting*
people to see you
when they *lack* **vision.**

To change your *thoughts,* **change what you** *consume.*

— *Alex Hormozi*

Happiness is conditional. Joy is accompanied by *everlasting* peace.

Trials *teach* **us what we are. They** *dig* **up the soil and let us see what we are** *made* **of.**

—*Charles Spurgeon*

God **never requires anything of His** *creation* **that He didn't already build into them.**

— *Myles Munroe*

Each *life*
is made up of
mistakes and learning,
waiting and growing,
practicing patience and
***being* persistent.**

— Billy Graham

When
it's *real,*
you can't
walk **away.**

— *Unknown.*

The *quieter* you become, the more you are able to *hear*.

— *Rumi*

Why *wish* upon a star when you can *pray* to the One who created it.

— *thisislovelifequotes.net*

Loyalty **is rare.**
If you find it, *keep* **it.**

— Unknown

You must be *honest* with yourself before *you* can be honest with others.

Forgiveness
is all the closure
you *need.*

Our *unrealistic expectations* break our hearts before another person does.

Raise your words,
not your voice.
It is rain that grows
flowers, not thunder.

— Rumi

Sometimes, *healing* requires *action*. Other times, it requires *rest*.

Don't let
regret **be your**
constant *companion.*

Not *everyone*
can receive care,
compassion,
consideration and love.
Give it to
them *anyway.*

God's **purpose is more important than our** *plans.*

— *Myles Munroe*

The most *radical* growth takes *place* when no one is looking.

We need
to *confront* **our past**
in order to shake hands
with our *future.*

Difficult roads *lead* to *beautiful* destinations.

— *Unknown*

One day, the *girl* with the books becomes the *woman* writing them.

— *Unknown*

Also by Talisha A Matheson

The Little Book of Introverted Thoughts – Vol 1

The Little Book of Introverted Thoughts – Vol 2

Soul Talks: 52-Weeks of Inspiration

www.ingramcontent.com/pod-product-compliance
Lightning Source LLC
Chambersburg PA
CBHW030906200726
48289CB00003B/915

9781777745387